JAZZ PIANO SOLOS   VOLUME 39

sacred christmas carols

Arranged by Brent Edstrom

contents

ISBN 978-1-4950-2735-2

HAL•LEONARD®
CORPORATION
7777 W. BLUEMOUND RD. P.O. BOX 13819 MILWAUKEE, WI 53213

In Australia Contact:
Hal Leonard Australia Pty. Ltd.
4 Lentara Court
Cheltenham, Victoria, 3192 Australia
Email: ausadmin@halleonard.com.au

Visit Hal Leonard Online at
www.halleonard.com

ANGELS FROM THE REALMS OF GLORY

Words by JAMES MONTGOMERY
Music by HENRY T. SMART

ANGELS WE HAVE HEARD ON HIGH

Traditional French Carol
Translated by JAMES CHADWICK

AS WITH GLADNESS MEN OF OLD

Words by WILLIAM CHATTERTON DIX
Music by CONRAD KOCHER

AWAY IN A MANGER

Words by JOHN T. McFARLAND (v.3)
Music by JAMES R. MURRAY

CHRIST WAS BORN ON CHRISTMAS DAY

Traditional

COME, THOU LONG-EXPECTED JESUS

Words by CHARLES WESLEY
Music by ROWLAND HUGH PRICHARD

COVENTRY CAROL

Words by ROBERT CROO
Traditional English Melody

DECK THE HALL

Traditional Welsh Carol

DING DONG! MERRILY ON HIGH!

French Carol

GO, TELL IT ON THE MOUNTAIN

African-American Spiritual
Verses by JOHN W. WORK, JR.

GOD REST YE MERRY, GENTLEMEN

19th Century English Carol

GOOD CHRISTIAN MEN, REJOICE

14th Century Latin Text
Translated by JOHN MASON NEALE
14th Century German Melody

Bright Swing

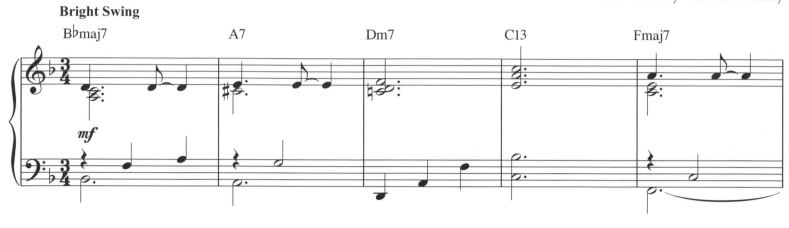

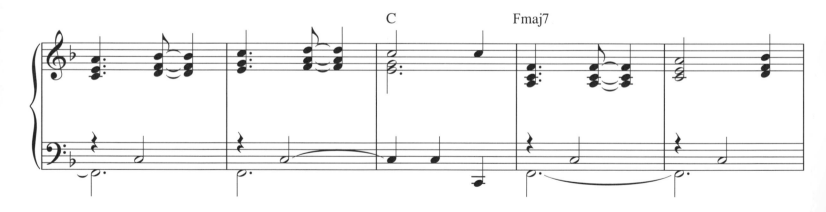

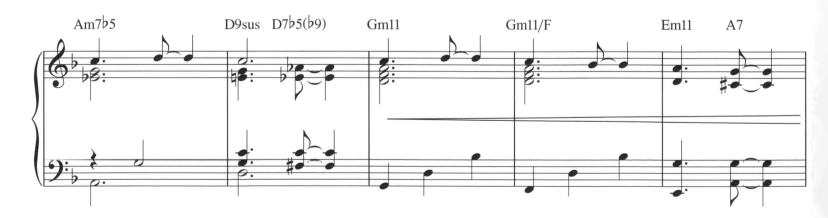

GOOD KING WENCESLAS

Words by JOHN M. NEALE
Music from *Piae Cantiones*

45

HARK! THE HERALD ANGELS SING

Words by CHARLES WESLEY
Altered by GEORGE WHITEFIELD
Music by FELIX MENDELSSOHN-BARTHOLDY
Arranged by WILLIAM H. CUMMINGS

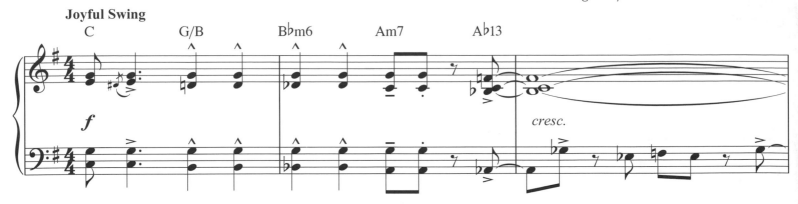

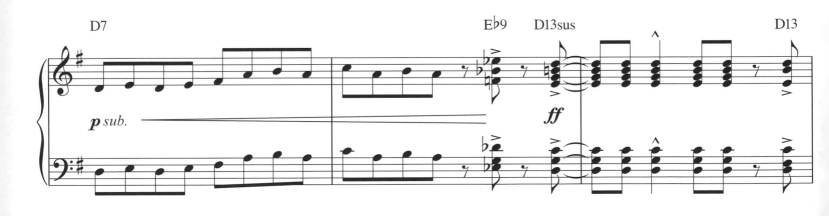

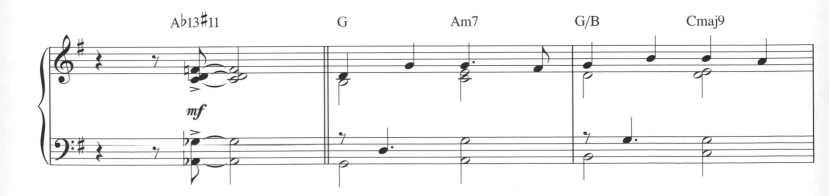

47

THE HOLLY AND THE IVY

18th Century English Carol

52

IN THE BLEAK MIDWINTER

Poem by CHRISTINA ROSSETTI
Music by GUSTAV HOLST

THE HURON CAROL

Traditional French-Canadian Text
Traditional Canadian-Indian Melody

To Coda ⊕

IT CAME UPON THE MIDNIGHT CLEAR

Words by EDMUND HAMILTON SEARS
Music by RICHARD STORRS WILLIS

62

JOY TO THE WORLD

Words by ISAAC WATTS
Music by GEORGE FRIDERIC HANDEL
Adapted by LOWELL MASON

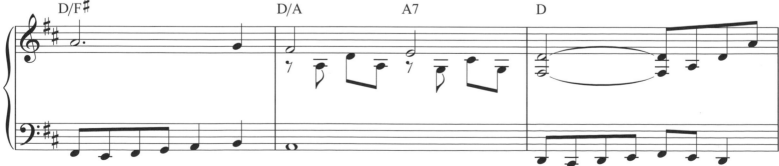

O COME, ALL YE FAITHFUL
(Adeste Fideles)

Music by JOHN FRANCIS WADE
Latin Words translated by FREDERICK OAKELEY

Relaxed Gospel Swing feel

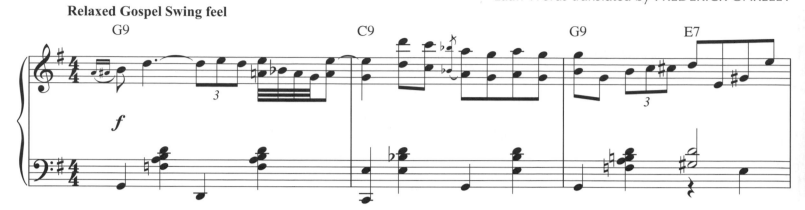

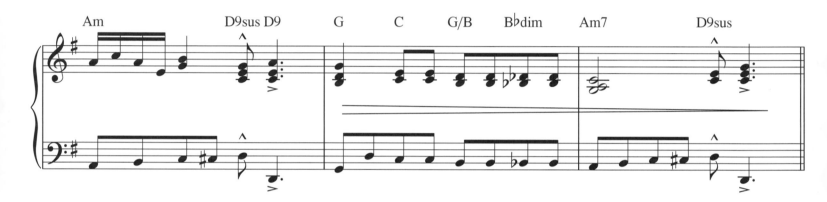

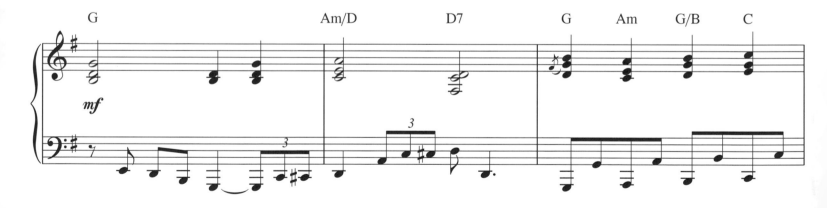

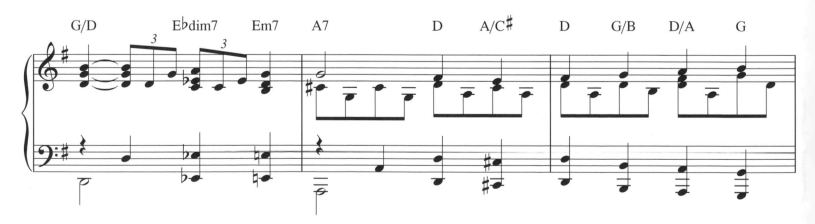

O COME, O COME IMMANUEL

Plainsong, 13th Century
Words translated by JOHN M. NEALE
and HENRY S. COFFIN

Delicate straight-8ths groove

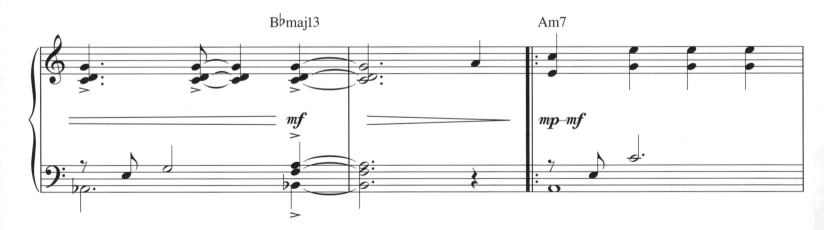

O HOLY NIGHT

French Words by PLACIDE CAPPEAU
English Words by JOHN S. DWIGHT
Music by ADOLPHE ADAM

O LITTLE TOWN OF BETHLEHEM

Words by PHILLIPS BROOKS
Music by LEWIS H. REDNER

Gentle Ballad

82

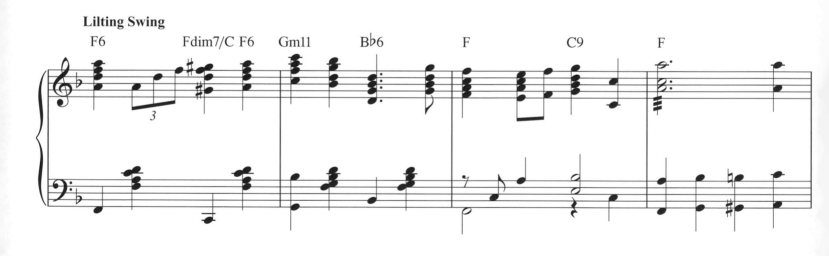

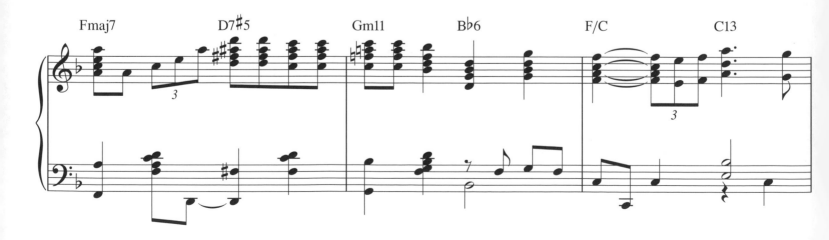

83

SILENT NIGHT

Words by JOSEPH MOHR
Translated by JOHN F. YOUNG
Music by FRANZ X. GRUBER

Moderately slow Swing

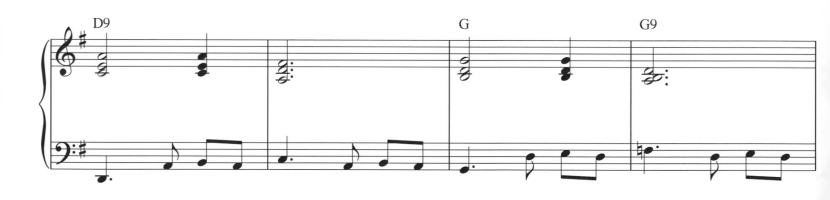

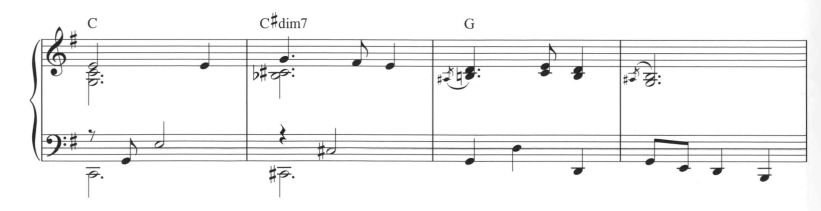

STILL, STILL, STILL

Salzburg Melody, c.1819
Traditional Austrian Text

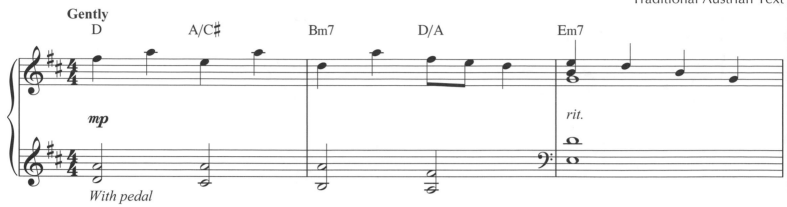

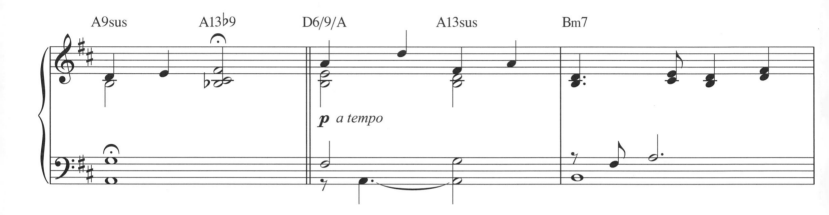

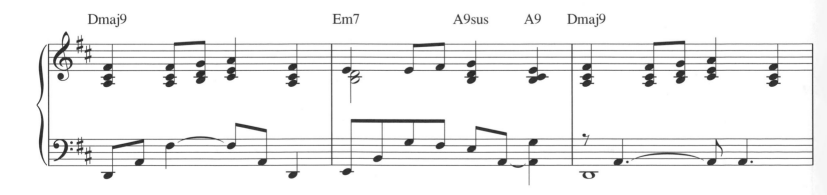

89

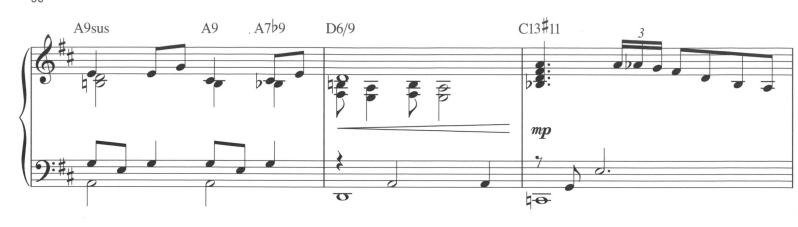

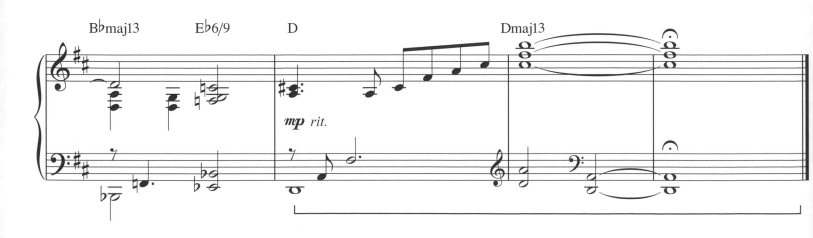

WE THREE KINGS OF ORIENT ARE

Words and Music by
JOHN H. HOPKINS, JR.

WHAT CHILD IS THIS?

Words by WILLIAM C. DIX
16th Century English Melody